WHAT HAPPENS WHEN CHRISTIANS LIVE LIKE CHRISTIANS

CHIP INGRAM

WHAT HAPPENS WHEN CHRISTIANS
LIVE LIKE CHRISTIANS

Table of Contents

How to Start Your Own Small Group

The fact that you are even reading this page says a lot about you. It says that you are either one of those people that has to read everything, or it says you are open to God using you to lead a group.

Leading a small group can sound intimidating, but it really doesn't have to be. Think of it more as gathering a few friends to get to know each other better and to have some discussion around biblical truths.

Here are a few practical tips to help you get started:

1. **Pray** – One of the most important principles of spiritual leadership is to realize you can't do this on your own. No matter how long you've been a Christian or been involved in ministry, you need the power of the Holy Spirit. Lean on Him... He will help you.

2. **Invite some friends** – Don't be afraid to ask people to come to your group. You will be surprised how many people are open to a study like this. Whether you have 4 or 14 in your group, it can be a powerful experience. You should probably plan on at least an hour and a half for your group meeting.

3. **Get your materials** – You will need to get a DVD of the video teaching done by Chip Ingram. You can get the DVD from livingontheedge.org. Also, it will be helpful for each person to have their own study guide. You can also purchase those through the Living on the Edge website.

4. **Be prepared to facilitate** – Just a few minutes a week in preparation can make a huge difference in the group experience. Each week, preview the video teaching and review the discussion questions. If you don't think your group can get through all the questions, select the ones that are most relevant to your group.

6. **Learn to say "I don't know."** – When tough questions come up, it's ok for you to say "I don't know." Take the pressure off. No one expects you to have all the answers.

7. **Love your group** – Maybe the most important thing you bring to the group is your personal care for them. If you will pray for them, encourage them, call them, email them, involve them, and love them, God will be pleased and you will have a lot of fun along the way.

Thank you for your availability. May God bless you as you serve Him by serving others.

How to Get the Most Out of This Experience

This small group series, taken from the book of Titus, is designed to help us know how to "do good" and make the Gospel attractive in our generation. In order to get the most out of this series, you will have to make the decision to dive in and engage this material.

Listed below are the segments you will experience each week as well as some hints for getting the most out of this experience. If you are leading the group, you will find some additional help and coaching tips on pages 70 - 73. Video coaching is also available under the Coaching menu on the DVD as well as at livingontheedge.org. Click "Small Groups and Coaching."

1. **Watch the Video** – It is important for us to get "before God" and submit ourselves to His truth. During this section you will watch the video teaching by Chip.

   A teaching outline with fill-ins is provided for each session. As you follow along, write down questions or insights that you can share during the discussion time.

   Even though most of the verses will appear on the screen and in your notes, it is a great idea to bring your own Bible each week. It will allow you to make notes in your own Bible and find other passages that might be relevant to that week's study.

2. **Talk It Over** – We not only grow by listening to God's Word, but we grow "in community." The friendship and insights of those in the group will enrich your small group experience. Several discussion questions are provided for your group to further engage the teaching content. Keep the following guidelines in mind for having a healthy group discussion.

   - Be involved. Jump in and share your thoughts. Your ideas are important, and you have a perspective that is unique and can benefit the other group members.

   - Be a good listener. Value what others are sharing. Seek to really understand the perspective of others in your group and don't be afraid to ask follow up questions.

   - Be courteous. Spirited discussion is great. Disrespect and attack is not. When there is disagreement, focus on the issue and never turn the discussion into a personal attack.

   - Be focused. Stay on topic. Help the group explore the subject at hand, and try to save unrelated questions or stories for afterwards.

- Be careful not to dominate. Be aware of the amount of talking you are doing in proportion to the rest of the group, and make space for others to speak.

- Be a learner. Stay sensitive to what God might be wanting to teach you through the lesson, as well as through what others have to say. Focus more on your own growth rather than making a point or winning an argument.

3. **Live It Out** – BIO is a word that is synonymous with "life." Found in those 3 simple letters B.I.O. is the key to helping you become the person God wants you to be.

   B = Come **"Before God"** daily – To meet with Him personally through His Word and prayer, to enjoy His presence, receive His direction, and follow His will.

   I = Do Life **"In Community"** weekly – Structuring your week to personally connect in safe relationships that provide love, support, transparency, challenge, and accountability.

   O = Be **"On Mission"** 24/7 – Cultivating a mindset to "live out" Jesus' love for others through acts of sacrifice and service at home, work, play, and church.

4. **Accelerate (20 minutes that turn concepts into convictions)**

Inspiration comes from hearing God's Word; **motivation** grows by discussing God's Word; **transformation** occurs when you study it for yourself.

If you want to "accelerate" your growth, a short Bible study is provided that you can do at home each week. Our convictions become even stronger when we dig into Scripture and discover truth for ourselves. To help you get the most out of this exercise, consider partnering up with somebody in your group who will also commit to do the assignment this week. Then, after you have each done the assignment, agree to spend 10-15 minutes by phone to share what you learned and what you are applying.

Session 1

Why Doing Good Matters So Much

Part 1

Take It In (Watch the Video)

Why DOING GOOD Matters So Much

The Book of Titus

Introduction – A Troubled Church – "Then & Now"

- The Church's Problems
    1. Believers' lives don't match their beliefs.
    2. Believers' conduct is discrediting their message.
    3. False Teachers are ruining families and destroying the Church.
- The Pastor's Assignment
    1. Straighten out the mess.
    2. Teach sound doctrine.
    3. Confront error and transform cities by DOING GOOD.
- The Underlying Issue
    1. If we are "saved by grace" totally apart from our good works, what difference does it make if we DO GOOD or not?

Titus Chapter 1 – DOING GOOD in the Church

- Author and Purpose *(v. 1-3)*
    1. From Apostle Paul
    2. For the faith of God's chosen people and the knowledge of the truth that leads to Godliness
    3. Based on our hope of eternal life in Jesus Christ
- Titus' Assignment #1 *(v. 4-9)*
    1. Set things in order and appoint godly leaders
    2. A leader must be...
        a. Blameless in marriage and family
        b. Blameless in character

        c. Hospitable, loves what's good, self-controlled, upright, holy, disciplined

        d. Theologically sound and able to guard the truth

- The Reason *(v. 10-16)*

    1. False teachers, deceivers, mere talkers, ruining whole families, dishonest, promoting Cretan vs. Christian values

    2. They claim to know God but by their deeds they deny Him

SUMMARY They're unfit for doing anything good. *(v. 16)*

Titus Chapter 2 – DOING GOOD in Relationships

- Titus' Assignment #2 *(v. 1-10)*

    1. Teach what "good" looks like in daily life to...

        a. Older men

        b. Older women

        c. Younger women

        d. Younger men

        e. Slaves

    2. Specific Results *(v. 5, 8, 10)*

- A Theology of "Doing Good" *(v. 11-14)*

For the grace of God has appeared that offers salvation to all people. It teaches us to say "No" to ungodliness and worldly passions, and to live self-controlled, upright and godly lives in this present age, while we wait for the blessed hope–the appearing of the glory of our great God and Savior, Jesus Christ, who gave himself for us to redeem us from all wickedness and to purify for himself a people that are his very own, eager to do what is good.

Titus 2:11-14 (NIV)

SUMMARY These are the things that you should teach. *(v. 15)*

Titus Chapter 3 – DOING GOOD in the Word

- Titus' Assignment #3 *(v. 1-2)*
  1. Remind God's people to...
     a. Submit to authorities
     b. Be ready to do whatever is good
     c. Slander no one
     d. Be peaceable and considerate
     e. Show true humility to ALL MEN
  2. The reason to Do Good to All *(v. 3-4)*
     a. Our past life
     b. Our new life by God's grace demands a new lifestyle!
- A Theology of "Becoming Good" *(v. 5-8)*
  1. Not by "works"
  2. Regeneration by His mercy to a "new birth"
  3. Justified by grace
- Warnings and Instructions *(v. 9-15)*
  1. Avoid foolish controversies
  2. Warn a divisive person
  3. Send co-workers, help others

SUMMARY	Our people must learn to devote themselves to doing what is good. *(v. 14)*

4 Reasons...

Why "Doing Good" Matters So Much *(2:11-14)*

1. Doing Good reveals God's ____________________ for all people. *(v. 11)*

   Key Concept = Salvation by grace *(Ephesians 2:4-9)*

   Application = Matthew 5:16 –

   ________________ ________________________ !

Talk It Over

1. Who is the greatest Christian you know? And in your opinion, what about them makes them a great Christian?

2. Chip talked about 3 specific problems the church at Crete had. What are some problems you observe in the church today that are a concern for you?

3. Chip said that the message of Christ and our "doing good" is rooted in the word grace. What does it mean to "do good" from a place of grace?

4. If you decided to get really serious about "doing good," what might change in how you live?

Live It Out – B.I.O.

BIO is a word that is synonymous with "life." Found in those 3 simple letters B.I.O. is the key to helping you become the person God wants you to be.

B = Come **Before God** daily – To meet with Him personally through His Word and prayer, to enjoy His presence, receive His direction, and follow His will.

I = Do Life **In Community** weekly – Structuring your week to personally connect in safe relationships that provide love, support, transparency, challenge, and accountability.

O = Be **On Mission** 24/7 – Cultivating a mindset to "live out" Jesus' love for others through acts of sacrifice and service at home, work, play, and church.

Come Before God

5. Titus 1:10-16 talks about "false teachers." Read the passage and discuss what makes someone a "false teacher?"

____

____

____

Do Life In Community

6. In Titus 2, Paul said that the grace of God helps us to say "no" to unrighteousness. Place an X on the line that would most accurately describe you.

I have no one honestly speaking into my life. — I have a person or two that honestly speak into my life.

Is this something you sincerely desire? What fears or barriers hold you back from pursuing this more?

____

____

Be On Mission

7. Chip challenged us to "shine brightly." As you think about your life, in what way could you let the light of Christ shine more brightly to those around you?

Accelerate (20 Minutes That Turns Concepts Into Convictions)

Inspiration comes from hearing God's Word; **motivation** grows by discussing God's Word; **transformation** occurs when you study it for yourself.

If you want to "accelerate" your growth, here is an assignment you can do this week. To help you get the most out of this exercise, consider partnering up with somebody in your group who will also commit to do the assignment this week. Then, after you have each done the assignment, agree to spend 10 minutes by phone to share what you learned and what you are applying.

Come Before God

1. The story of the Good Samaritan is a great passage about "doing good." Read the following passage through a couple of times. Read it slowly, really paying attention to words and phrases that jump out at you.

   On one occasion an expert in the law stood up to test Jesus. "Teacher," he asked, "what must I do to inherit eternal life?"

   "What is written in the Law?" he replied. "How do you read it?"

   He answered, "'Love the Lord your God with all your heart and with all your soul and with all your strength and with all your mind'; and, 'Love your neighbor as yourself.'"

   "You have answered correctly," Jesus replied. "Do this and you will live."

   But he wanted to justify himself, so he asked Jesus, "And who is my neighbor?" In reply Jesus said: "A man was going down from Jerusalem to Jericho, when he was attacked by robbers. They stripped him of his clothes, beat him and went away, leaving him half dead. A priest happened to be going down the same road, and when he saw the man, he passed by on the other side. So too, a Levite, when he came to the place and saw him, passed by on the other side. But a Samaritan, as he traveled, came where the man was; and when he saw him, he took pity on him. He went to him and bandaged his wounds, pouring on oil and wine. Then he put the man on his own donkey, brought him to an inn and took care of him. The next day he took out two denarii and gave them to the innkeeper. 'Look after him,' he said, 'and when I return, I will reimburse you for any extra expense you may have.'

"Which of these three do you think was a neighbor to the man who fell into the hands of robbers?"

The expert in the law replied, "The one who had mercy on him." Jesus told him, "Go and do likewise."

Luke 10:25-37 (NIV)

2. When this man asks Jesus what he must do to inherit eternal life, why do you think Jesus responds with "What is written in the Law?"

____

____

____

3. From verses 33-35, make a list of practical things the Samaritan did to help this man in need.

-
-
-
-
-

4. What were some of the "costs" involved in being a "good Samaritan"?

5. Based on this story, how would you answer the question "who is my neighbor?"

Do Life In Community

6. Get together with someone in your small group or another friend this week and talk about ways that you could be more like the Good Samaritan.

Be On Mission

7. This week look for an opportunity to move outside your comfort zone and be a "good Samaritan" to somebody that crosses your path.

Session 2

Why Doing Good Matters So Much

Part 2

Take It In (Watch the Video)

4 Reasons...

Why "Doing Good" Matters So Much

Titus 2:11-14

From last week's lesson...

1. Doing Good reveals God's **PASSION** for all people. *(v. 11)*

2. Doing Good reveals Christ's ______________________ in our lives. *(v. 12)*

   Key Concept = Grace produces life change *(Matthew 7:15-23)*

   Application = 2 Corinthians 13:5 –

   ______________________ ______________________!

3. Doing Good reveals the ______________________ of our lives. *(v. 13)*

   Key Concept = Live with an eternal perspective *(Philippians 3:17-21)*

   Application = Matthew 25:1-13 –

   ______________________ ______________________!

4. Doing Good reveals Jesus' ______________________ for our lives. *(v. 14)*

   Key Concept = You are His workmanship *(Ephesians 2:10)*

   Application = John 15:8 –

   ______________ ______________ ______________!

Talk It Over

1. Who in your life has sacrificially "done good" to you? What did they do and how did it impact you?

2. When you become a Christian, God begins to change your desires. As you have come to know Christ, what are some desires that he has changed or taken away?

3. Titus 2 says that our relationship with God teaches us how to live "self-controlled." What does it mean for you to live a "self-controlled" life? Be specific and practical.

4. Chip talked about the difference between a temporal and eternal perspective. What would it look like to live from an eternal perspective?

Live It Out – B.I.O.

BIO is a word that is synonymous with "life." Found in those 3 simple letters B.I.O. is the key to helping you become the person God wants you to be.

B = Come **Before God** daily – To meet with Him personally through His Word and prayer, to enjoy His presence, receive His direction, and follow His will.

I = Do Life **In Community** weekly – Structuring your week to personally connect in safe relationships that provide love, support, transparency, challenge, and accountability.

O = Be **On Mission** 24/7 – Cultivating a mindset to "live out" Jesus' love for others through acts of sacrifice and service at home, work, play, and church.

Come Before God

5. Read Philippians 3:17-21. How should the fact that our citizenship is in heaven motivate us to "do good"?

____

____

____

Do Life In Community

6. In Titus 2, Paul says that our encounter with grace teaches us to live "upright." This is about how we relate to other people. What is one way your group could pray for you as you seek to live "upright" in your relationships?

____

____

____

Be On Mission

7. Chip challenged us for 7 days to do good for those in our world. Share with your group one specific person you will commit to "do good" for this next week.

____

____

____

Accelerate (20 Minutes That Turns Concepts Into Convictions)

Inspiration comes from hearing God's Word; **motivation** grows by discussing God's Word; **transformation** occurs when you study it for yourself.

If you want to "accelerate" your growth, here is an assignment you can do this week. To help you get the most out of this exercise, consider partnering up with somebody in your group who will also commit to do the assignment this week. Then, after you have each done the assignment, agree to spend 10 minutes by phone to share what you learned and what you are applying.

Come Before God

1. Read the following passage from Ephesians 2 carefully and slowly. Read it through a couple of times paying attention to key words and phrases.

   As for you, you were dead in your transgressions and sins, in which you used to live when you followed the ways of this world and of the ruler of the kingdom of the air, the spirit who is now at work in those who are disobedient. All of us also lived among them at one time, gratifying the cravings of our flesh and following its desires and thoughts. Like the rest, we were by nature deserving of wrath. But because of his great love for us, God, who is rich in mercy, made us alive with Christ even when we were dead in transgressions–it is by grace you have been saved. And God raised us up with Christ and seated us with him in the heavenly realms in Christ Jesus, in order that in the coming ages he might show the incomparable riches of his grace, expressed in his kindness to us in Christ Jesus. For it is by grace you have been saved, through faith–and this is not from yourselves, it is the gift of God–not by works, so that no one can boast. For we are God's handiwork, created in Christ Jesus to do good works, which God prepared in advance for us to do.

   Ephesians 2:1-10 (NIV)

2. In verses 1-3, as you read about your life before Christ, what stands out to you the most? Why?

___

___

___

3. What does Paul mean in verse 6 when he says "God raised us up with Christ and seated us with him in the heavenly realms"?

___

___

___

4. In verse 10, Paul says that we are God's "handiwork created in Christ Jesus to do good works." Take a moment to reflect on God's good work in your life and then write out what you believe are the "good works" God has for you to do.

___

___

___

Do Life In Community

5. This week share with someone your personal testimony. Share how you came to Christ, the changes He has made in your life, and how He is currently working in your life.

Be On Mission

6. Who is someone you know who hasn't yet experienced the life-changing power of the gospel? Commit to pray for them each day this week and look for an opportunity to share the good news with them.

Session 3

Doing Good – Where It All Begins

Part 1

Take It In (Watch the Video)

DOING GOOD – Where It All Begins

Titus Chapter 1

Introduction – The Power of DOING GOOD

- It pushes back the darkness.
- It rescues people from destruction.
- It connects our hearts to others.
- It provides unexplainable joy.

Review – Why DOING GOOD Matters So Much

1. DOING GOOD reveals God's **passion** for people.
2. DOING GOOD reveals God's **presence** in our lives.
3. DOING GOOD reveals the **priority** of our lives.
4. DOING GOOD reveals God's **purpose** for our lives.

Question – *If DOING GOOD honors God, helps others, and transforms me... where do I begin to become a person who habitually DOES GOOD?*

Doing good begins by recognizing who ____________________ what is good. *(v. 1-4)*

- By what authority?

- By what standard?

- For what purpose?

I. DOING GOOD in an organization always begins with the

________________________________ *(v. 5-16)*

- Appoint ____________________ leaders. *(v. 5-9)*
- Remove __________________ leaders. *(v. 10-16)*
- Refuse to ______________________________. *(v. 12)*

II. DOING GOOD personally begins with ____________________ you are, not what you ___________. *(v.5-16)*

Talk It Over

1. Who is a leader that you respect and what is it about them that you respect and admire?

____

____

____

2. In Chip's introduction he talked about the fact that Doing Good…
   - pushes back the darkness
   - rescues people from destruction
   - connects our hearts to others
   - provides unexplainable joy

   Share a personal story where you experienced one of those 4 results of Doing Good.

3. God's standard for leadership in the church are very high. What are some of the consequences or fallout when a leader doesn't live up to those standards?

4. When Paul talks about leadership, he puts the focus on character and not skill or technique. How do you feel leadership and the qualifications for leadership has shifted in the last 25-30 years?

Live It Out – B.I.O.

BIO is a word that is synonymous with "life." Found in those 3 simple letters B.I.O. is the key to helping you become the person God wants you to be.

B = Come **Before God** daily – To meet with Him personally through His Word and prayer, to enjoy His presence, receive His direction, and follow His will.

I = Do Life **In Community** weekly – Structuring your week to personally connect in safe relationships that provide love, support, transparency, challenge, and accountability.

O = Be **On Mission** 24/7 – Cultivating a mindset to "live out" Jesus' love for others through acts of sacrifice and service at home, work, play, and church.

Come Before God

5. Review Titus 1:5-9. What most stands out to you about the qualities of a godly leader? Which of the qualities in verses 5-9 do you feel like you do possess and which one do you think you need to work on?

6. Review Titus 1:10-16. What should we learn from this passage about removing bad leaders?

Do Life In Community

7. Share one way that this group could help you be a better leader?

Be On Mission

8. It takes tremendous courage to be a godly leader in our culture. Spend a few minutes as a group praying for leaders in your church and community.

Accelerate (20 Minutes That Turns Concepts Into Convictions)

Inspiration comes from hearing God's Word; **motivation** grows by discussing God's Word; **transformation** occurs when you study it for yourself.

If you want to "accelerate" your growth, here is an assignment you can do this week. To help you get the most out of this exercise, consider partnering up with somebody in your group who will also commit to do the assignment this week. Then, after you have each done the assignment, agree to spend 10 minutes by phone to share what you learned and what you are applying.

Come Before God

1. Read through the following passage a couple of times.

    After the death of Moses the servant of the LORD, the LORD said to Joshua son of Nun, Moses' aide: "Moses my servant is dead. Now then, you and all these people, get ready to cross the Jordan River into the land I am about to give to them—to the Israelites. I will give you every place where you set your foot, as I promised Moses. Your territory will extend from the desert to Lebanon, and from the great river, the Euphrates—all the Hittite country—to the Mediterranean Sea in the west. No one will be able to stand against you all the days of your life. As I was with Moses, so I will be with you; I will never leave you nor forsake you. Be strong and courageous, because you will lead these people to inherit the land I swore to their ancestors to give them.

    "Be strong and very courageous. Be careful to obey all the law my servant Moses gave you; do not turn from it to the right or to the left, that you may be successful wherever you go. Keep this Book of the Law always on your lips; meditate on it day and night, so that you may be careful to do everything written in it. Then you will be prosperous and successful. Have I not commanded you? Be strong and courageous. Do not be afraid; do not be discouraged, for the LORD your God will be with you wherever you go."

    Joshua 1:1-9 (NIV)

2. How do you think Joshua must have felt having to follow Moses as a leader? What would you have felt?

3. What did God say to Joshua that would give him confidence to lead?

4. From verse 6-9, what leadership insights do you discover that would be helpful for anyone stepping into a leadership role?

Do Life In Community

5. Share with someone in your small group or another friend what you learned from this passage about leadership. Also share with them one area that you want to grow as a leader.

Be On Mission

6. Several times God would tell Joshua "be strong and very courageous." As you think about your life, where do you need to be more courageous? What would it look like practically to be more courageous in that area?

Session 4

Doing Good – Where It All Begins

Part 2

Take It In (Watch the Video)

III. DOING GOOD personally begins with who you are, not what you do.
(*Titus 1:5-16)*

- Qualifications for leaders/people to DO GOOD.

1. ***Character*** = __________________

2. ***At Home*** = Devoted and Discipling

3. ***Relationally*** = Emotionally Mature

    a. Not addicted to __________________ .

    b. Not controlled by anger.

    c. Not dependant on __________________ .

    d. Not leading with coercion.

4. ***Ministry Mindset*** = Outwardly Focused

    a. A lover of __________________ .

    b. Devoted to kindness.

5. ***Private World*** = __________________ with self, others and God in thought, word and deed.

6. ***Motives and Methods*** = Pure, teachable, __________________!

Talk It Over

1. Which one of the qualities we talked about in this session most stands in contrast to leadership we often see in our culture? And share "why" you think that.

2. What is one way that you could "step up" your spiritual leadership at home, church, or on the job? If you have kids, how can you do a better job of spiritually leading your children?

3. Chip said that good leaders are emotionally mature. When a leader is emotionally immature, what are some of the effects on those they lead?

4. Spend a few minutes as a group reflecting on the life of Jesus. What characteristics and behaviors marked his leadership?

Live It Out – B.I.O.

BIO is a word that is synonymous with "life." Found in those 3 simple letters B.I.O. is the key to helping you become the person God wants you to be.

B = Come **Before God** daily – To meet with Him personally through His Word and prayer, to enjoy His presence, receive His direction, and follow His will.

I = Do Life **In Community** weekly – Structuring your week to personally connect in safe relationships that provide love, support, transparency, challenge, and accountability.

O = Be **On Mission** 24/7 – Cultivating a mindset to "live out" Jesus' love for others through acts of sacrifice and service at home, work, play, and church.

Come Before God

5. James 4:4 says, *You adulterous people, don't you know that friendship with the world means enmity against God? Therefore, anyone who chooses to be a friend of the world becomes an enemy of God.*

   Chip said that godly leaders not only love what is good, but they hate what is evil. As a Christian living in the 21st century, what does it look like practically to hate evil and be separate from the world?

   ____

   ____

   ____

Do Life In Community

6. How could your group pray for you as a leader?

   ____

   ____

   ____

Be On Mission

7. Good leaders are hospitable and devoted to kindness. What are some practical ways that you could show hospitality and kindness to those in your world?

____

____

____

Accelerate (20 Minutes That Turns Concepts Into Convictions)

Inspiration comes from hearing God's Word; **motivation** grows by discussing God's Word; **transformation** occurs when you study it for yourself.

If you want to "accelerate" your growth, here is an assignment you can do this week. To help you get the most out of this exercise, consider partnering up with somebody in your group who will also commit to do the assignment this week. Then, after you have each done the assignment, agree to spend 10 minutes by phone to share what you learned and what you are applying.

Come Before God

1. Read the following passage from 1 Peter 5 a couple of times. This is a great passage on godly leadership, so look for key words and phrases that stand out to you.

   To the elders among you, I appeal as a fellow elder and a witness of Christ's sufferings who also will share in the glory to be revealed: Be shepherds of God's flock that is under your care, watching over them—not because you must, but because you are willing, as God wants you to be; not pursuing dishonest gain, but eager to serve; not lording it over those entrusted to you, but being examples to the flock. And when the Chief Shepherd appears, you will receive the crown of glory that will never fade away.

   In the same way, you who are younger, submit yourselves to your elders. All of you, clothe yourselves with humility toward one another, because,

   "God opposes the proud but shows favor to the humble."

Humble yourselves, therefore, under God's mighty hand, that he may lift you up in due time. Cast all your anxiety on him because he cares for you.

Be alert and of sober mind. Your enemy the devil prowls around like a roaring lion looking for someone to devour. Resist him, standing firm in the faith, because you know that the family of believers throughout the world is undergoing the same kind of sufferings.

And the God of all grace, who called you to his eternal glory in Christ, after you have suffered a little while, will himself restore you and make you strong, firm and steadfast. To him be the power for ever and ever. Amen.

1 Peter 5:1-11 (NIV)

2. Of all the metaphors God could have chosen to speak of godly leadership, why do you think he chooses the metaphor of "shepherd"?

____

____

____

3. Take a few moments to contrast the world's way of leading people and God's way of leading people.

The World's Way	**God's Way**
1.	1.
2.	2.
3.	3.
4.	4.
5.	5.

4. Peter talks about humble leadership. List out some practices and characteristics of "humble leadership"

    •

    •

    •

    •

Do Life In Community

5. Get together with a friend this week and spend some time praying for those who are leaders in your life... i.e. your pastor, your small group leader, your boss.

Be On Mission

6. 1 Pete 5:7 says "Cast your anxiety on him, because he cares for you." When it comes to your own leadership, what are you anxious about? What is a barrier that keeps you from leading like 1 Peter 5?

   Spend some time in prayer casting your anxiety on God and asking for his power to lead well.

Session 5

The High Cost of Not Doing Good

Part 1

Take It In (Watch the Video)

The High Cost of Not DOING GOOD

Titus Chapter 2

Introduction – DOING GOOD Looks Different for Different People, but...

1. DOING GOOD is not a suggestion.
2. DOING GOOD is powerful.
3. DOING GOOD can be risky.
4. DOING GOOD begins with character not our conduct.

The price of DOING GOOD can be ____________________________!

The price of not DOING GOOD can be more __________________!

- Barna study on Christian families
- Barna study on Spiritual engagement in America
- Barna study on perception of Christians in America

At home?

1. **Older Men** are to be...
   - Temperate
   - Worth of respect
   - Self-controlled
   - Healthy in faith, love and endurance
2. **Older Women** are...
   - Reverent in the way of life
   - Not to be slanderers
   - Not to be addicted to much wine

- Teach what is good
- Teach younger women

3. **Younger Women** are to...

- Love their husbands and children
- Be self controlled and pure
- Be busy at home and be kind

Why? – So that God's Word will not be ______________________!

Talk It Over

1. Who is an older man or woman that you respect? And what is it about them that you respect?

____

____

____

2. In the book Unchristian, the author says, "Christians in America today are viewed as harsh, judgmental, intolerant, anti-intellectual, and hypocritical."How do you respond to such an assessment and how do we change the perception of Christians?

____

____

____

3. In the last 30 years, how have we seen attitudes shift toward those who are older? And, how has that impacted the church?

___

___

___

4. In Titus 2:4-5, Paul talks about older women mentoring younger women. If you were going to mentor a young man or young woman, what are a couple of things you would want to pass down to them?

___

___

___

Live It Out – B.I.O.

BIO is a word that is synonymous with "life." Found in those 3 simple letters B.I.O. is the key to helping you become the person God wants you to be.

B = Come **Before God** daily – To meet with Him personally through His Word and prayer, to enjoy His presence, receive His direction, and follow His will.

I = Do Life **In Community** weekly – Structuring your week to personally connect in safe relationships that provide love, support, transparency, challenge, and accountability.

O = Be **On Mission** 24/7 – Cultivating a mindset to "live out" Jesus' love for others through acts of sacrifice and service at home, work, play, and church.

Come Before God

5. Titus 2:1-5 says, *You, however, must teach what is appropriate to sound doctrine. Teach the older men to be temperate, worthy of respect, self-controlled, and sound in faith, in love and in endurance. Likewise, teach the older women to be reverent in the way they live, not to be slanderers or addicted to much wine, but to teach what is good. Then they can urge the younger*

women to love their husbands and children, to be self-controlled and pure, to be busy at home, to be kind, and to be subject to their husbands, so that no one will malign the word of God.

As you get older, what qualities listed of older men and older women do you especially want to be true of you? Why?

____

____

____

Do Life In Community

6. As you hear the phrase "finish well," what does that mean for you personally? Share some of your longings and desires for "finishing well."

   Then, break up into prayer partners and pray for the longings and desires that have been mentioned.

____

____

____

Be On Mission

7. This week, what older man or older woman could you honor and encourage? How will you do that?

____

____

____

Accelerate (20 Minutes That Turns Concepts Into Convictions)

Inspiration comes from hearing God's Word; **motivation** grows by discussing God's Word; **transformation** occurs when you study it for yourself.

If you want to "accelerate" your growth, here is an assignment you can do this week. To help you get the most out of this exercise, consider partnering up with somebody in your group who will also commit to do the assignment this week. Then, after you have each done the assignment, agree to spend 10 minutes by phone to share what you learned and what you are applying.

Come Before God

1. Read the following passage from Joshua 14 a couple of times.

   Now the people of Judah approached Joshua at Gilgal, and Caleb son of Jephunneh the Kenizzite said to him, "You know what the LORD said to Moses the man of God at Kadesh Barnea about you and me. I was forty years old when Moses the servant of the LORD sent me from Kadesh Barnea to explore the land. And I brought him back a report according to my convictions, but my fellow Israelites who went up with me made the hearts of the people melt in fear. I, however, followed the LORD my God wholeheartedly. So on that day Moses swore to me, 'The land on which your feet have walked will be your inheritance and that of your children forever, because you have followed the LORD my God wholeheartedly.'

   "Now then, just as the LORD promised, he has kept me alive for forty-five years since the time he said this to Moses, while Israel moved about in the wilderness. So here I am today, eighty-five years old! I am still as strong today as the day Moses sent me out; I'm just as vigorous to go out to battle now as I was then. Now give me this hill country that the LORD promised me that day. You yourself heard then that the Anakites were there and their cities were large and fortified, but, the LORD helping me, I will drive them out just as he said."

   Then Joshua blessed Caleb son of Jephunneh and gave him Hebron as his inheritance. So Hebron has belonged to Caleb son of Jephunneh the Kenizzite ever since, because he followed the LORD, the God of Israel, wholeheartedly.

   Joshua 14:6-14 (NIV)

2. In verse 8, Caleb tells Joshua that he had followed the Lord "wholeheartedly." What is the evidence from this passage that Caleb had followed God "wholeheartedly"?

____

____

____

3. Go through this passage and underline all the statements or phrases that indicate Caleb was still a man of faith and ambition, even at the age of 85.

4. Look up the following verses and write down what wholehearted devotion looks like in these verses.

    - Ephesians 6:7 ____________________________________
    - 2 Kings 20:3 ____________________________________
    - 1 Chronicles 28:9 ________________________________
    - 1 Chronicles 29:9 ________________________________
    - 1 Chronicles 29:19________________________________

Do Life In Community

5. Spend some time reflecting on this passage from Joshua 14. Then write out what kind of old person you want to be and share it with a friend or family member.

Be On Mission

6. Think of an older person that you respect and invite them to lunch. Make it a point to learn from their life experiences and wisdom.

Session 6

The High Cost of Not Doing Good

Part 2

Take It In (Watch the Video)

4. **Younger Men** are to... *(Titus Chapter 2)*

    - Be self-controlled
    - Follow Titus' example and teaching

Why? – So that critics may have no basis for their accusations about

_____________ _____________________.

At work?
Slaves of both Christian and non Christian masters are to...

- Be subject to their masters
- Try to please (satisfy) them
- Not talk back to them
- Not steal from them
- Show they can be trusted

Why? – So that in every way they will make the teaching about God our Savior

___________________________.

3 Questions to Stimulate Your Faith:

1. What has the power to convince an unbelieving world that God's Word is true?
2. What has the power to restore credibility and influence to the Church?
3. What has the power to make people want to explore a personal relationship with Jesus Christ?

The Answer to all 3 = Doing Good where you ________________

and where you ________________.

Talk It Over

1. When you think of your life, what could you actually do that would make the gospel more attractive to your friends, neighbors, and co-workers?

2. When you hear the phrase "Christians living like Christians," what comes to mind?

3. In our homes and in our churches, how do you think we are doing with teaching young men "self-control"? What are some ways that we could help young men in their journey of self-control?

4. Paul challenged Titus to set a good example for the younger men who were looking up to him. Who in your life was a good role model for spiritual maturity? How did they impact you?

Live It Out – B.I.O.

BIO is a word that is synonymous with "life." Found in those 3 simple letters B.I.O. is the key to helping you become the person God wants you to be.

B = Come **Before God** daily – To meet with Him personally through His Word and prayer, to enjoy His presence, receive His direction, and follow His will.

I = Do Life **In Community** weekly – Structuring your week to personally connect in safe relationships that provide love, support, transparency, challenge, and accountability.

O = Be **On Mission** 24/7 – Cultivating a mindset to "live out" Jesus' love for others through acts of sacrifice and service at home, work, play, and church.

Come Before God

5. Read Titus 2:9-10, Ephesians 6:5-9 and Colossians 3:22-24. Even though these passages are written to slaves, there is much that applies to us in the workplace. What insights from this passage inform how we are to function in our work environment?

___

___

___

Do Life In Community

6. Paul calls on us to make the gospel "attractive." But we know that we can also make the gospel "unattractive." Where in your life or work can you "blow it" and possibly be a stumbling block to others? Share that with your group and allow them to hold you accountable in that area.

___

___

___

Be On Mission

7. What is one thing you will commit to doing this week that will make the gospel more attractive to those you encounter?

Accelerate (20 Minutes That Turns Concepts Into Convictions)

Inspiration comes from hearing God's Word; **motivation** grows by discussing God's Word; **transformation** occurs when you study it for yourself.

If you want to "accelerate" your growth, here is an assignment you can do this week. To help you get the most out of this exercise, consider partnering up with somebody in your group who will also commit to do the assignment this week. Then, after you have each done the assignment, agree to spend 10 minutes by phone to share what you learned and what you are applying.

Come Before God

1. Carefully read the following passages from Ephesians and Colossians:

   Slaves, obey your earthly masters with respect and fear, and with sincerity of heart, just as you would obey Christ. Obey them not only to win their favor when their eye is on you, but as slaves of Christ, doing the will of God from your heart. Serve wholeheartedly, as if you were serving the Lord, not people, because you know that the Lord will reward each one for whatever good they do, whether they are slave or free.

   Ephesians 6:5-8 (NIV)

   Slaves, obey your earthly masters in everything; and do it, not only when their eye is on you and to curry their favor, but with sincerity of heart and reverence for the Lord. Whatever you do, work at it with all your heart, as working for the Lord, not for human masters, since you know that you will receive an inheritance from the Lord as a reward. It is the Lord Christ you are serving.

   Colossians 3:22-24 (NIV)

2. Even though this passage was written to slaves, it can certainly apply to us and the attitude we are to have when doing our jobs.

   Why do you think Paul tells us to obey our masters or employers with "fear"?

   ____

   ____

   ____

3. In Ephesians 6:8 Paul says that God will "reward" each one for whatever good they do. What kind of reward is Paul referring to?

   ____

   ____

   ____

4. What does it mean to do your work with "reverence for the Lord"? (Colossians 3:22)

   ____

   ____

   ____

Do Life In Community

5. Spend some time this week talking with a friend about your job and how you can better live out the principles taught in Ephesians 6 and Colossians 3.

Be On Mission

6. If you were to work this month as if Jesus were your boss, how would you do your job differently?

Session 7

How Doing Good Will Change Your World

Part 1

Take It In (Watch the Video)

Introduction – There's Hope for Your Community *(Titus Chapter 3)*

1. What has the power to convince your neighbors, friends, and co-workers that God's Word is true?

2. What has the power to restore your credibility and influence as a follower of Christ?

3. What has the power to make your neighbors, friends, and co-workers want to explore a personal relationship with Jesus Christ?

The Answer to all 3 = DOING GOOD in your home, at your work and in

your ______________________ .

For You In Your Community? *(v. 1-2)*

1. Obey the ______________ . – Romans 13:7
   - *"submit to rulers and authority"*
2. Serve your ____________________ . – Galatians 6:10
   - *"ready to do whatever is good"*
3. Guard your________________ . – Ephesians 4:29
   - *"slander no one"*
4. Refuse to______________ . – Romans 12:17-18
   - *"be peaceable" (literally a "non-fighter")*

5. Be ______________________________ and forbearing. – James 3:17

    • *"be considerate, gentle, willing to yield one's rights"*

6. Treat everyone like a ___________ – Philippians 2:3-4

    • *"show yourself humble to all men"*

Talk It Over

1. Who in your past has treated you like a VIP? What did they do that made you feel like a VIP, and how did it impact you?

____

____

____

2. Read Romans 13:1-7. What insights do you have from this passage that speak to how Christians should view and interact with government?

____

____

____

3. Paul calls on us to "be peaceable" which is literally translated "be a non-fighter." And Chip challenged us to take our stand with grace. What would that look like practically? Can you think of a situation where you might need to take a stand on something, but do it with grace?

____

____

____

4. Chip said, "We are not trying to win a cultural war... we are trying to win people's hearts." How do you respond to his statement? And what are the implications of that statement for Christians and churches?

____

____

____

Live It Out - B.I.O.

BIO is a word that is synonymous with "life." Found in those 3 simple letters B.I.O. is the key to helping you become the person God wants you to be.

B = Come **Before God** daily - To meet with Him personally through His Word and prayer, to enjoy His presence, receive His direction, and follow His will.

I = Do Life **In Community** weekly - Structuring your week to personally connect in safe relationships that provide love, support, transparency, challenge, and accountability.

O = Be **On Mission** 24/7 - Cultivating a mindset to "live out" Jesus' love for others through acts of sacrifice and service at home, work, play, and church.

Come Before God

5. Read 1 Peter 2:18-25. What can we learn from Jesus about gentleness and giving up our rights?

____

____

____

Do Life In Community

6. One of the ways we make the gospel attractive is to serve our community. Spend a few minutes talking about a way your group could serve your local community. Create a plan for serving your community together, as a group.

Be On Mission

7. According to Paul, we make the gospel attractive by being considerate and by not slandering. As you think about your world, where do you tend to be negative (critical) and how could you be more considerate?

____

____

____

Accelerate (20 Minutes That Turns Concepts Into Convictions)

Inspiration comes from hearing God's Word; **motivation** grows by discussing God's Word; **transformation** occurs when you study it for yourself.

If you want to "accelerate" your growth, here is an assignment you can do this week. To help you get the most out of this exercise, consider partnering up with somebody in your group who will also commit to do the assignment this week. Then, after you have each done the assignment, agree to spend 10 minutes by phone to share what you learned and what you are applying.

Come Before God

1. Read this passage from Daniel 1 and try to imagine yourself as a teenager placed in this kind of situation.

   In the third year of the reign of Jehoiakim king of Judah, Nebuchadnezzar king of Babylon came to Jerusalem and besieged it. And the Lord delivered Jehoiakim king of Judah into his hand, along with some of the articles from the temple of God. These he carried off to the temple of his god in Babylonia and put in the treasure house of his god.

   Then the king ordered Ashpenaz, chief of his court officials, to bring into the king's service some of the Israelites from the royal family and the nobility—young men without any physical defect, handsome, showing aptitude for every kind of learning, well informed, quick to understand, and qualified to serve in the king's palace. He was to teach them the language and literature of the Babylonians. The king assigned them a daily amount of food and wine from the king's table. They were to be trained for three years, and after that they were to enter the king's service.

Among those who were chosen were some from Judah: Daniel, Hananiah, Mishael and Azariah. The chief official gave them new names: to Daniel, the name Belteshazzar; to Hananiah, Shadrach; to Mishael, Meshach; and to Azariah, Abednego.

But Daniel resolved not to defile himself with the royal food and wine, and he asked the chief official for permission not to defile himself this way. Now God had caused the official to show favor and compassion to Daniel, but the official told Daniel, "I am afraid of my lord the king, who has assigned your food and drink. Why should he see you looking worse than the other young men your age? The king would then have my head because of you."

Daniel then said to the guard whom the chief official had appointed over Daniel, Hananiah, Mishael and Azariah, "Please test your servants for ten days: Give us nothing but vegetables to eat and water to drink. Then compare our appearance with that of the young men who eat the royal food, and treat your servants in accordance with what you see." So he agreed to this and tested them for ten days.

At the end of the ten days they looked healthier and better nourished than any of the young men who ate the royal food. So the guard took away their choice food and the wine they were to drink and gave them vegetables instead.

To these four young men God gave knowledge and understanding of all kinds of literature and learning. And Daniel could understand visions and dreams of all kinds.

Daniel 1:1-17 (NIV)

2. According to verses 3-4, what were some of the qualities of these young men placed in king Nebuchadnezzar's court?

____

____

____

3. In Daniel 1:8 the Bible says, "Daniel resolved not to defile himself." How do you think a person develops that kind of resolve? Who are some other biblical characters that resolved to take a stand?

4. What can we learn from Daniel's approach to "taking a stand" for his beliefs?

Do Life In Community

5. Find a friend this week who will memorize Proverbs 11:3 with you. In this verse, Solomon says "The integrity of the upright guides them, but the unfaithful are destroyed by their duplicity." Check in with each other a couple of times and quote the verse to each other.

Be On Mission

6. Where in your life do you need to "take a stand"? What practical steps can you take?

Session 8

How Doing Good Will Change Your World

Part 2

Take It In (Watch the Video)

Why Must We "Do Good" In Our Communities? *(Titus Chapter 3)*

1. Because our _____________ __________ demands we __________ . *(v. 3)*
   - *"we were foolish, disobedient, deceived, enslaved..."*

2. Because our _________ ____________ demands we ___________ . *(v. 4-8)*
   - The divine intervention = He ______________ us! *(v. 4-5)*
   - The ________________ of our salvation. *(v. 6)*
     - *"not by works of righteousness we have done"*
     - *but according to His mercy He saved us"*
   - The ______________ of our salvation. *(v. 6)*
     - *"by the washing of regeneration"*
     - *"by the renewing of the Holy Spirit"*
   - The __________________ of our salvation. *(v. 7-8)*
     1. A New Standing Before God
     2. A New Future With God
     3. A New Mandate From God

A Final Word to Titus *(v. 9-15)*

1. A New Standing Before God
2. A New Future With God
3. A New Mandate From God

THE BIG IDEA	Our people must learn to DEVOTE themselves to DOING GOOD.

Talk It Over

1. Share with your group a time when you physically got lost... how did it feel? What emotions did you experience?

2. What was your former life like before Christ and how has He transformed you?

3. If we are going to "do good" we must learn not to be judgmental. Honestly, where are you tempted to be judgmental and how can you protect your heart from a judgmental spirit?

4. Being baptized is an act of obedience by publicly declaring your faith in Jesus. If you have been baptized, share what that meant to you. If you haven't been baptized, is there something keeping you from taking this next step?

Live It Out – B.I.O.

BIO is a word that is synonymous with "life." Found in those 3 simple letters B.I.O. is the key to helping you become the person God wants you to be.

B = Come **Before God** daily – To meet with Him personally through His Word and prayer, to enjoy His presence, receive His direction, and follow His will.

I = Do Life **In Community** weekly – Structuring your week to personally connect in safe relationships that provide love, support, transparency, challenge, and accountability.

O = Be **On Mission** 24/7 – Cultivating a mindset to "live out" Jesus' love for others through acts of sacrifice and service at home, work, play, and church.

Come Before God

5. Once you receive Christ, you have access to every spiritual blessing. Read Ephesians 1:3-14 and make a list of all the blessings you now have in Christ.

____

____

____

Do Life In Community

6. Share with your group how this series has impacted you and what is your one big "take-away" from this study?

Be On Mission

7. Chip spoke about doing radical, sacrificial, extravagant good. Spend a few minutes brainstorming and dreaming about ways you could do "extravagant good."

____

____

____

Accelerate (20 Minutes That Turns Concepts Into Convictions)

Inspiration comes from hearing God's Word; **motivation** grows by discussing God's Word; **transformation** occurs when you study it for yourself.

If you want to "accelerate" your growth, here is an assignment you can do this week. To help you get the most out of this exercise, consider partnering up with somebody in your group who will also commit to do the assignment this week. Then, after you have each done the assignment, agree to spend 10 minutes by phone to share what you learned and what you are applying.

Come Before God

1. Read this great story from 2 Samuel 9 a couple of times.

   David asked, "Is there anyone still left of the house of Saul to whom I can show kindness for Jonathan's sake?"

   Now there was a servant of Saul's household named Ziba. They summoned him to appear before David, and the king said to him, "Are you Ziba?"

   "At your service," he replied.

   The king asked, "Is there no one still alive from the house of Saul to whom I can show God's kindness?"

   Ziba answered the king, "There is still a son of Jonathan; he is lame in both feet."

   "Where is he?" the king asked.

   Ziba answered, "He is at the house of Makir son of Ammiel in Lo Debar."

   So King David had him brought from Lo Debar, from the house of Makir son of Ammiel.

   When Mephibosheth son of Jonathan, the son of Saul, came to David, he bowed down to pay him honor.

   David said, "Mephibosheth!"

   "At your service," he replied.

"Don't be afraid," David said to him, "for I will surely show you kindness for the sake of your father Jonathan. I will restore to you all the land that belonged to your grandfather Saul, and you will always eat at my table."

Mephibosheth bowed down and said, "What is your servant, that you should notice a dead dog like me?"

Then the king summoned Ziba, Saul's steward, and said to him, "I have given your master's grandson everything that belonged to Saul and his family. You and your sons and your servants are to farm the land for him and bring in the crops, so that your master's grandson may be provided for. And Mephibosheth, grandson of your master, will always eat at my table." (Now Ziba had fifteen sons and twenty servants.)

Then Ziba said to the king, "Your servant will do whatever my lord the king commands his servant to do." So Mephibosheth ate at David's table like one of the king's sons.

Mephibosheth had a young son named Mika, and all the members of Ziba's household were servants of Mephibosheth. And Mephibosheth lived in Jerusalem, because he always ate at the king's table; he was lame in both feet.

---

2 Samuel 9:1-13 (NIV)

2. Go through the passage and underline any words or phrases that speak of kindness and grace.

3. Why in verse 8, do you think Mephibosheth's response is to say "What is your servant that you should notice a dead dog like me?"

____

____

____

4. Ephesians 1:7-8a says, *In him we have redemption through his blood, the forgiveness of sins, in accordance with the riches of God's grace that he lavished on us.*

   How is David's treatment of Mephibosheth a good picture of the grace that God lavished on us?

   ____

   ____

   ____

Do Life In Community

5. Where do you have the most trouble showing grace? Have a conversation with a friend about this question and then spend some time praying for one another.

Be On Mission

6. One of the ways that we show grace is by being "gracious." Make it a point this week to be extravagantly "gracious."

Small Group Leader Resources

Group Agreement

People come to groups with a variety of different expectations. The purpose of a group agreement is simply to make sure everyone is on the same page and that we have some common expectations.

The following Group Agreement is a tool to help you discuss specific guidelines during your first meeting. Modify anything that does not work for your group. Then be sure to discuss the questions in the section called Our Game Plan. This will help you to have an even better group experience!

We Agree To The Following Priorities:

Take the Bible Seriously	To seek to understand and apply God's truth in the Bible
Group Attendance	To give priority to the group meeting (call if I am going to be absent or late)
Safe Environment	To create a safe place where people can be heard and feel loved (no snap judgments or simple fixes)
Respectful Discussion	To speak in a respectful and honoring way to our mate and others in the group
Be Confidential	To keep anything that is shared strictly confidential and within the group
Spiritual Health	To give group members permission to help me live a godly, healthy spiritual life that is pleasing to God
Building Relationships	To get to know the other members of the group and pray for them regularly
Pursue B.I.O.	To encourage and challenge each other in "coming before God," "doing life together in community," and "being on mission 24/7"
Prayer	To regularly pray with and for each other
Other	______________________________

Our game plan:

1. What day and time will we meet? ______________________________

2. Where will we meet? ______________________________

3. How long will we meet each week? ______________________________

4. What will we do for refreshments? ______________________________

5. What will we do about childcare? ______________________________

Tips for Facilitating Your Group Meeting

Before the group arrives

1. **Be prepared.** Your personal preparation can make a huge difference in the quality of the group experience. We strongly suggest previewing both the DVD teaching by Chip Ingram and the study guide.

2. **Pray for your group members by name.** Ask God to use your time together to touch the heart of every person in your group. Expect God to challenge and change people as a result of this study.

3. **Provide refreshments.** There's nothing like food to help a group relax and connect with each other. For the first week, we suggest you prepare a snack, but after that, ask other group members to bring the food so that they share in the responsibilities of the group and make a commitment to return.

4. **Relax.** Don't try to imitate someone else's style of leading a group. Lead the group in a way that fits your style and temperament. Remember that people may feel nervous showing up for a small group study, so put them at ease when they arrive. Make sure to have all the details covered prior to your group meeting, so that once people start arriving, you can focus on them.

Take It In (Watch the Video)

1. Get the video ready. Each video session will be between 15 and 20 minutes in length. Go ahead and cue up the video so that you can just push "play" when you are ready to watch the session.

2. Have ample materials. Before you start the video, also make sure everyone has their own study guide. Encourage the group to open to this week's session and follow along with the teaching. There is an outline in the study guide with an opportunity to fill in the outline.

3. Arrange the room. Set up the chairs in the room so that everyone can see the television. And, arrange the room in such a way that it is conducive to discussion.

Talk It Over

Here are some guidelines for leading the discussion time:

1. **Make this a discussion, not a lecture.** Resist the temptation to do all the talking, and to answer your own questions. Don't be afraid of a few moments of silence while people formulate their answers.

   And don't feel like you need to have all the answers. There is nothing wrong with simply saying "I don't know the answer to that, but I'll see if I can find an answer this week."

2. **Encourage everyone to participate.** Don't let one person dominate, but also don't pressure quieter members to speak during the first couple of sessions. Be patient. Ask good follow up questions and be sensitive to delicate issues.

3. **Affirm people's participation and input.** If an answer is clearly wrong, ask "What led you to that conclusion?" or ask what the rest of the group thinks. If a disagreement arises, don't be too quick to shut it down! The discussion can draw out important perspectives, and if you can't resolve it there, suggest researching it further and return to the issue next week.

   However, if someone goes on the offensive and engages in personal attack, you will need to step in as the leader. In the midst of spirited discussion, we must also remember that people are fragile and there is no place for disrespect.

4. **Detour when necessary.** If an important question is raised that is not in the study guide, take time to discuss it. Also, if someone shares something personal and emotional, take time for them. Stop and pray for them right then. Allow the Holy Spirit room to maneuver, and follow His prompting when the discussion changes direction.

5. **Subgroup.** One of the principles of small group life is "when numbers go up, sharing goes down." So, if you have a large group, sometimes you may want

to split up into groups of 4-6 for the discussion time. This is a great way to give everyone, even the quieter members, a chance to share. Choose someone in the group to guide each of the smaller groups through the discussion. This involves others in the leadership of the group, and provides an opportunity for training new leaders.

6. **Prayer.** Be sensitive to the fact that some people in your group may be uncomfortable praying out loud. As a general rule, don't call on people to pray unless you have asked them ahead of time or have heard them pray in public. But this can also be a time to help people build their confidence to pray in a group. Consider having prayer times that ask people to just say a word or sentence of thanks to God.

Live It Out – B.I.O.

At this point in each week's session, you will engage the B.I.O. pathway. B.I.O. is a process that is designed to help Christians live like Christians. As you integrate these three vital practices into your life, it will result in spiritual momentum and help you thrive as a follower of Jesus.

- **Come "Before God" Daily** - To meet with Him personally through His Word and prayer, in order to enjoy His Presence, receive His direction, and follow His will.
- **Do Life "In Community" Weekly** - Structuring your week to personally connect in safe relationships that provide love, support, transparency, challenge, and accountability.
- **Be "On Mission" 24/7** - Cultivating a mindset to "live out" Jesus love for others through acts of sacrifice and service at home, work, play and church.

Accelerate (20 minutes that turns concepts into convictions)

Inspiration comes from hearing God's Word; **motivation** grows by discussing God's Word; **transformation** occurs when you study it for yourself.

This 20 minute exercise is meant to be done apart from the group meeting. It is a great way to go deeper with the material and turbo charge people's growth. You can lead the way by doing personally doing the Accelerate section each week. And then encourage others to join and take a few moments in your group meeting to talk about what people have been learning from this section.

Doing Good Session Notes

Welcome to this series called Doing Good. When Christians "do good" and actually live like Christians, we give greater credibility to the gospel. And when Christians say one thing and live another, we undermine the credibility of the gospel.

Whether you are brand new at leading a small group or you are a seasoned veteran, God is going to use you. God has a long history of using ordinary people to get His work done.

These brief notes are intended to help prepare you for each week's session. By spending just a few minutes each week previewing the video and going over these session notes, you will set the table for a great group experience. Also, don't forget to pray for your group each week.

Session 1 – Why Doing Good Matters So Much, Pt. 1

- If your group doesn't know each other well, be sure that you spend some time getting acquainted. Don't rush right into the video lesson. Remember, small groups are not just about a study or a meeting, they are about relationships.
- Be sure to capture everyone's contact information. It is a good idea to send out an e-mail with everybody's contact information so that the group can stay in touch. At the back of your study guide is a roster where people can fill in the names and contact information of the other group members.
- When you are ready to start the session, be sure that each person in your group has a study guide. The small group study guide is important for people to follow along and to take notes.
- Spend a little time in this first session talking about B.I.O. These 3 core practices are the pathway to maturity. You will see these letters and terms throughout this curriculum. Start getting your group comfortable with the concepts of "coming before God," "doing life together in community," and "being on mission."
- Facilitating the discussion time. Sometimes Chip will ask you as the facilitator to lead the way by answering the first question. This allows you to lead by example and your willingness to share openly about your life will help others feel the permission to do the same.

- Before you wrap up your group time, be sure to introduce the Accelerate exercise in the study guide. This is an assignment they can do during the week that will help turbo charge their growth. Encourage them to find a partner in the group who they can talk to each week about the accelerate exercise.

- The concept of Doing Good is a simple idea. Help your group understand that we are not talking about just being polite, or nice, or kind, or considerate. No, we are talking about radical good. The kind of good that will make the gospel attractive.

- Question 2 in study guide this week will ask "what are some problems you observe in the church today that are a concern for you? Don't let this turn into church bashing. And don't let people begin to attack their church or another church in the community. Let this discussion be about specific issues facing the church in general.

Session 2 – Why Doing Good Matters So Much, Pt. 2

- Why not begin your preparation by praying right now for the people in your group. You might even want to keep their names in your Bible. You may also want to ask people in your group how you can pray for them specifically.

- If somebody doesn't come back this week, be sure and follow up with them. Even if you knew they were going to have to miss the group meeting, give them a call or shoot them an e-mail letting them know that they were missed. It would also be appropriate to have a couple of other people in the group let them know they were missed.

- If you haven't already previewed the video, take the time to do so. It will help you know how to best facilitate the group and what are the best discussion questions for your group.

- Ask good follow up questions... the only thing better than a good question is a good follow up question. Think of your group discussion like an onion. Each good follow up question allows you to pull back another lay and go beneath the surface.

- During the teaching, Chip will present a 7 day challenge for doing good at home or on the job. He will encourage your group to find a way to remind themselves of this challenge... like wearing your watch on the opposite wrist. Ask each group member what their reminder will be?

- Chip will say that "the most dangerous position is a religious person who has never truly been born again." And then he will share the gospel... he will encourage anyone that made the decision to follow Christ to talk to you the group leader. So, if that happens...
    - Encourage and affirm their decision. Celebrate them taking this step.
    - Connect them to Living on the Edge where they can get additional resources that will help them get started in their faith.
    - Personally follow up with them in the next few days.

Session 3 - Doing Good – Where It All Begins, Pt. 1

- Did anybody miss last week's session? If so, make it a priority to follow up and let them know they were missed. It just might be your care for them that keeps them connected to the group.
- Don't be afraid of silence. We don't like dead time, do we? It makes us feel uncomfortable. To be a good facilitator, you must learn to get comfortable with silence. Silence gives people a moment to process and figure out what they want to say. If you move on too quickly, you miss some of the best input.
- Think about last week's meeting for a moment. Was there anyone that didn't talk or participate? In every group there are extroverts and there are introverts. There are people who like to talk and then there are those who are quite content NOT to talk. Not everyone engages in the same way or at the same level, but you do want to try and create an environment where everyone wants to participate.
- Follow up with your group this week to see how they did with the Accelerate assignment this week. Don't shame or embarrass anyone who didn't get to the assignment, but honestly challenge them to make this a priority in the coming week.
- As you begin your group time this week, follow up on the 7 day challenge. Take some time to have people share how it went. There will be some who just got busy and it fell off the radar... encourage them to take the challenge again this week.
- This is a lesson about leadership in the church. Some in the group will think this doesn't apply to them. They don't see themselves as leaders, but the truth is that we all have people we influence. So, these principles are valuable for every person in your group.

- At the end of the session Chip will challenge some in you group to step into places of leadership. They could do this at home, church, community, or in your small group. So, be prepared. Idenitfy where you could use some help.

Session 4 – Doing Good — Where It All Begins, Pt. 2

- Don't feel pressure to get through all the questions. As people open up and talk, don't move on too quickly. Give them the space to open up to what is going on inside them as they interact with this teaching.
- Share the load. One of the ways to raise the sense of ownership within the group is to get others involved in more than just coming to the meetings. So, get someone to help with refreshments... find somebody else to be in charge of the prayer requests... get someone else to be in charge of any social gathering you plan... let someone else lead the discussion one night. Give away as much of the responsibility as possible. That is GOOD leadership.
- If your group is not sharing as much as you would like or if the discussion is being dominated by a person or two, try subgrouping. If your group is 8 people or more, this is a great way to up the level of participation. After watching the video teaching, divide the group into a couple of smaller groups for the discussion time. It is good to get someone you think would be a good facilitator to agree to this ahead of time.

Session 5 – The High Cost of Not Doing Good, Pt. 1

- You are now at the halfway point of this series. How is it going? How well is the group connecting? What has been going well and what needs a little work? Are there any adjustments you need to make?
- Confidentiality is crucial to group life. The moment trust is breached, people will shut down and close up. So, you may want to mention the importance of confidentiality again this week, just to keep it on people's radar.
- Each time your group meets, take a few minutes to update what has happened since the last group meeting. Ask people what they are learning and putting into practice. Remember, being a disciple of Jesus means becoming a "doer of the Word."
- Revisit the importance of B.I.O. this week. Reinforce the importance of people integrating these core practices in their lives. For example, talk

about the priority of coming before God each day and submitting to the authority of God's truth.

- Don't chase rabbits. This happens in every group. You will ask a discussion and someone will take you down a trail that really isn't relevant to the discussion. It is your job as the group leader to discern when you need to bring the group back. Here is how I often handle that situation... I will look for a moment to jump in and say "Hey, this is great discussion but I want to come back to our topic and focus our discussion there."

- As you get started into your meeting this week follow up on the assignment from last week of people creating their "to be" list. For those who didn't work on it, challenge them again to take on this assignment. You might even want to send an e-mail reminder during the week.

- Chip will talk about how we are leading at home. Many of us are so busy chasing the American dream that we have little focus on our homes. "Perhaps for some of us, the big take-away from this lesson is that you need to sit down as a family and have a serious discussion about how you are living. Does your lifestyle really reflect God's priorities? And, where do you need to recalibrate your lives? "You might want to encourage couples to get a date night on the calendar where they can have this important discussion.

Session 6 – The High Cost of Not Doing Good, Pt. 2

- One way to deepen the level of community within your group is to spend time together outside the group meeting. If you have not already done so, plan something that will allow you to get to know each other better. Also, consider having someone else in the group take responsibility for your fellowship event.

- As you begin this week's session, do a check-in to see what people are learning and applying from this series. Don't be afraid to take some time at the beginning of your meeting to review some key ideas from the previous week's lessons.

- Consider asking someone in your group to facilitate next week's lesson. Who knows, there might be a great potential small group leader in your group. It will give you a break and give them a chance to grow.

- Your job is not to lead a good meeting. Your job is to help develop those in your group into mature followers of Jesus. So, encourage people to take a next step in their growth. Don't just ask them what they could do, ask them what they WILL do. We don't grow by talking about obedience, we grow by "obeying" and being "doers of the Word."

- Paul calls on us to make the gospel attractive… but the truth is we can also make the gospel "unattractive." So, in question #6 this week you will be asked "Where in your life or work can you blow it and possibly be a stumbling block to others?" This question is an opportunity to be vulnerable and transparent. It might be helpful for you to lead the way. Your own transparency will give others in the group permission to be transparent as well.

Session 7 – How Doing Good Will Change Your World, Pt. 1

- Consider sending an e-mail to each person in your group this week letting them know you prayed for them today. Also, let them know that you are grateful that they are in the group.
- Take a few minutes this week before you get into the study to talk about the impact of this series so far. Ask people what they are learning, applying, and changing in their lives. For this series to have lasting impact it has to be more than just absorbing information. So, challenge your group to put what they are learning into action.
- It is often a good idea to take a week break and do something different. This also helps the group understand that small group is more than just a meeting. You might consider taking one night off from your group meeting to just have dinner together and share/celebrate how God has used this series in your lives. Or, you could take a night off from your group meeting to do your ministry project and "do good" for someone in need.
- Since this is the next to the last week of this study, you might want to spend some time this week talking about what your group is going to do after your complete this study.
- Chip will ask your group to use their imagination and dream a little about what could happen if we got serious about "DOING GOOD." In your discussion time make sure that your group gets specific and practical about doing good. Dream about what might happen if every person in your group got serious about "doing good" in your community?
- In question 6 your group will be challenged to spend a few minutes talking about a way you could serve your local community. Don't just have a discussion, make a decision. And then create a plan for "doing good" in your local community.

Session 8 – How Doing Good Will Change Your World, Pt. 2

- "Thanks" for you willingness to lead this group... and thanks for your faithfulness in investing in those in your group. And I hope you have grown and been blessed by this material and by the people in your group.
- Be sure that everyone is clear what your group is doing next after this study.
- In question #3 this week it says "If we are going to "do good" we must learn not to be judgmental. Honestly, where are you tempted to be judgmental and how can you protect your heart from a judgmental spirit?" You might need to sit with some silence while people think about this question, it is an important one, so don't just rush past it.
- Question #4 says "Being baptized is an act of obedience in publicly declaring your faith in Jesus. If you have been baptized, share what that meant to you. If you haven't been baptized, is there something keeping you from taking this next step?" This can be a tricky question because different churches and denominations have differing views about baptism, both the theology of it and the practice. The important point is that baptism is a public declaration of a person's faith in Christ. For those who haven't been baptized, encourage them to study it biblically and to ask the Lord what they should do.
- Question #6 says... "Share with your group how this series has impacted you and what is your one big "take-away" from this study?" So, how can your group keep the momentum going and how can you encourage one another to continue to "do good"? One of the challenges with any small group series is how to sustain what we have learned once the series is over. So, spend a few minutes talking about this and commit to live out Hebrews 10:24 "And let us consider how we may spur one another on toward love and good deeds..."

Prayer and Praise

One of the most important things you can do in your group is to pray with and for each other. Write down each other's concerns here so you can remember to pray for these requests during the week!

Use the Follow Up box to record an answer to a prayer or to write down how you might want to follow up with the person making the request. This could be a phone call, an e-mail or a card. Your personal concern will mean a lot!

Date	Person	Prayer Request	Follow Up

Date	Person	Prayer Request	Follow Up

Date	Person	Prayer Request	Follow Up

Date	Person	Prayer Request	Follow Up

Date	Person	Prayer Request	Follow Up

Date	Person	Prayer Request	Follow Up

Date	Person	Prayer Request	Follow Up

Date	Person	Prayer Request	Follow Up

Date	Person	Prayer Request	Follow Up

Date	Person	Prayer Request	Follow Up

Date	Person	Prayer Request	Follow Up

Date	Person	Prayer Request	Follow Up

Group Roster

Name	Home Phone	Email

What's Next?

More Group Studies from Chip Ingram:

Balancing Life's Demands

Biblical Priorities for a Busy Life

Busy, tired and stressed out? Learn how to put "first things first" and find peace in the midst of pressure and adversity.

BIO

How to Become An Authentic Disciple of Jesus

Unlock the Biblical DNA for spiritual momentum by examining the questions at the heart of true spirituality.

Culture Shock

A Biblical Response to Today's Most Divisive Issues

Bring light–not heat–to divisive issues, such as abortion, homosexuality, sex, politics, the environment, politics and more.

Effective Parenting in a Defective World

Raising Kids that Stand Out from the Crowd

Packed with examples and advice for raising kids, this series presents Biblical principles for parenting that still work today.

Experiencing God's Dream for Your Marriage

Practical Tools for a Thriving Marriage

Examine God's design for marriage and the real life tools and practices that will transform it for a lifetime.

Five Lies that Ruin Relationships

Building Truth-Based Relationships

Uncover five powerful lies that wreck relationships and experience the freedom of understanding how to recognize God's truth.

The Genius of Generosity

Lessons from a Secret Pact Between Friends

The smartest financial move you can make is to invest in God's Kingdom. Learn His design for wise giving and generous living.

Watch previews and order at livingontheedge.org or 888.333.6003.

God As He Longs for You to See Him

Seeing God With 20/20 Vision

A deeper look at seven attributes of God's character that will change the way you think, pray and live.

Good to Great in God's Eyes

10 Practices Great Christians Have in Common

If you long for spiritual breakthrough, take a closer look at ten powerful practices that will rekindle a fresh infusion of faith.

Heaven

It's Not What You Think

Chip Ingram digs into scripture to reveal what heaven will be like, what we'll do there, and how we're to prepare for eternity today.

Holy Ambition

Turning God-Shaped Dreams Into Reality

Do you long to turn a God-inspired dream into reality? Learn how God uses everyday believers to accomplish extraordinary things.

House or Home: Marriage Edition

God's Blueprint for a Great Marriage

Get back to the blueprint and examine God's plan for marriages that last for a lifetime.

House or Home: Parenting Edition

God's Blueprint for Biblical Parenting

Timeless truths about God's blueprint for parenting, and the potential to forever change the trajectory of your family.

The Invisible War

The Believer's Guide to Satan, Demons and Spiritual Warfare

Learn how to clothe yourself with God's "spiritual armor" and be confident of victory over the enemy of your soul.

Watch previews and order at livingontheedge.org or 888.333.6003.

Love, Sex and Lasting Relationships

God's Prescription to Enhance Your Love Life

Do you believe in "true love"? Discover a better way to find love, stay in love, and build intimacy that lasts a lifetime.

Overcoming Emotions that Destroy

Constructive Tools for Destructive Emotions

We all struggle with destructive emotions that can ruin relationships. Learn God's plan to overcome angry feelings for good.

Rebuilding Your Broken World

How God Puts Broken Lives Back Together

Starting over? Learn how God can reshape your response to trials and bring healing to broken relationships and difficult circumstances.

Spiritual Simplicity

Doing Less • Loving More

If you crave simplicity and yearn for peace this study is for you. Spiritual simplicity can only occur when we do less and love more.

Transformed

The Miracle of Life Change

Ready to make a change? Explore God's process of true transformation and learn to spot barriers that hold you back from receiving God's best.

True Spirituality

Becoming a Romans 12 Christian

We live in a world that is activity-heavy and relationship-light. Learn the next steps toward True Spirituality.

Why I Believe

Answers to Life's Most Difficult Question

Can miracles be explained? Is there really a God? There are solid, logical answers about claims of the Christian faith.

Your Divine Design

Discover, Develop and Deploy Your Spiritual Gifts

How has God uniquely wired you? Discover God's purpose for spiritual gifts and how to identify your own.

Watch previews and order at livingontheedge.org or 888.333.6003.